NOISE IN THE FACE OF

NOISE IN THE FACE OF
David Buuck

David Buuck's *Noise in the Face of* is not a book exposing lies. It is about the labor of standing together in the face of the exposed and learning to be there for one another. There is Love here and there is a promise for enough of it, just stand in there and you know he is right. What an honor to be alive at the same time as this poet who is showing that there is so much more beyond the filth and conspiracy of politics.

—*CA Conrad*

David Buuck's *Noise in the Face of* amplifies the clamors and cries of the party of disorder as it faces the long-range acoustic devices of police phraseology. Tracing lines of solidarity that run counter to the clicks and swipes of 21st century capitalism, moving from the administrative transmissions of the police scanner to the nervous figuration of the rabble, *Noise in the Face of* gives us a 360-degree view of an antagonistic collective as it forms in the streets of Oakland and beyond. It reads our future in fire.

—*Jasper Bernes*

David Buuck writes a history of the problem of being a poet inside the historical moment of a city which itself had become a poem "sick of poetry, not finding another form for this roving disgust." Oakland was once a messed-up erupting ambiguity of the negatively capable indecorously accessorizing, the messed-up positron of the all, but maybe what Oakland was also was the precipice overlooking Silicon Valley, a cliff geo-tagged as a protest taking the form of a funeral in the form of a dance you refuse to do: "Whose fuck ups? / Our fuck ups." The meta-shards of mega-self-awareness that come after are a jewel on the radiant pavement of *after that*.

—*Anne Boyer*

NOISE IN THE FACE OF

David Buuck

ROOF BOOKS
NEW YORK

Cover art by Sophie Iremonger, "Neutron Bomb in Pleasure City" (detail).

NEW YORK STATE OF OPPORTUNITY. | Council on the Arts This book is made possible, in part, by the New York State Council on the Arts with the support of Governor Andrew Cuomo and the New York State Legislature.

Roof Books are distributed by
Small Press Distribution
1341 Seventh Street
Berkeley, CA. 94710-1403
Phone orders: 800-869-7553
www.spdbooks.org

Roof Books are published by
Segue Foundation
300 Bowery
New York, NY 10012
seguefoundation.com

CONTENTS

until all events speak for themselves
until representations know what it feels like
—Deanna Ferguson

for my friends in Oakland

Nothing has less street cred than representation
—Jeroen Mettes

CLEARING A SPACE IN THE FREQUENCY JUNGLE

What a century
for digits—the tips
of these fingers
tattooed with
decimal points
serving not
as endstops
but as pressure
points for inter-
faces to face
the screenfield
& press down
against the pulsing
stubs of some far-
away othersomes
whose hands
hardwired
my machine
tho I can't feel
her skinprints
through the plastics
that will end
up afloat
in the ocean
that lies
between us

like a container
ship loaded
with cool ranch
microchips RFID'd
to the longshoremen's
debit cards

It's this vision
of numbers
traipsing down
the screen
as we cram
into the seats
of the home
theater system
having paid
$89.99 a month
to watch time
unravel
to a beat
we call clock

Dancing along
to what I hate
most in my shelf
of cultured goods
sweatin' out the
contradictions
as the beer
cans tumble
somebody live
streams the scene

But I just don't
have the band-
width to handle
that right now
even as I spin
the ipod wheel
till I find Off
the Wall, street-
moves commence
down on the sticky
screaming—

We love you
Michael Jackson.
        Don't afraid.

        But I could barely hear we
                over the shoulds
    & should nots
                    of the blogosphere

        the entirety of
which was   literarily
        sitting in the armchair
                discarded outside
        the Oakland Museum

Boots.   Trampled grass.   Breaks between raids.
        Here where

        so much depends
                on the grey metal fence
                        enclosing the plaza

        Tis but a ruckus or a ruction
        Til the riot act's declared
        The fluid mass called crowd
        It pours and spreads
        Sluices and swells
        Gushes, trickles, and overflows
        It creeps and crawls, meanders and slips
        Waddles, loiters, lumbers and slides.

As affects are effects
Did not mean
to feel that
way back
on on on—tomorrow

When all's I want
is a temporary autonomous bouncy house
with a tinfoil canopy
so as to clear
      a space
      in the frequency—jungle

and block the NSA
from organizing my archives
provisionally titled A History
          of Dustbins.

While I'm inside   hitting refresh
      @ http://isoaklandburning.com

         Fueling the amped-up
         jacked from the streetlights

         dudes, let's bounce.

Then through the Y
to the why not us?

Snatch n Grab
drinks at Radio

staging area
for "the end

of the beginning"

       * * * * *

but not not not asynchronically jesterly—
not not not that guy, that t-shirt, that banner add-on—

not not not double-clicking on twinkle-finger icons—
not not not dude, cool ranch, really? I thought I said—
not not not soft snitch riot porn platforming—
not not not twitter wars as politics by other memes—
not not not your swabs, my spit, your DNA—machine—
not not not cross-linking my data capabilities to my forearm
  with a sharpie—
not not not the gluten-free wheat-paste contingency plank—
not not not oh,   here   come   the   puppets—
not not not ours or theirs—?

                I livestreamed it
                to myself   with my own fucking eyes
                        & then GIF'd that shit
                                out thru the aftermirth

        the glitter bloc
        at the docks
                inside the picket
                black flags
                gone rainbow

        on a map
        it's all vectors
                from staging
                ground to
                skirmish line

        the riot
        as rejection
                of existing
                forms of
                mediation

        the riot
        as crisis

of legitimation
come home
to roust

And never underestimate
        the power

of the black
        monochrome

stretched tight
        across a frame

or hanging from
        a wooden stick

        Cuz the revolution
        will not
        be funded

        but fueled
        by a stolen car battery
        powering the mobile
        sound system

        Cuz to dance
        in the street
        is the method

        Hurtling towards
        the absolute
        present

                We are not
                a photo-op.

This is not
my likeness.

& & &—No,

you accumulate me—or it does,
tallies my debt   burden
in future   labor   hours
I literally owe you my life-time,
or owe it, or whatever machine
licks the time stamp
& fixes the ink, or oil,
since I filled my printer
w/ top-shelf petroleum
to make a, y'know, a statement?
like smashing the copy machine
cuz we come from the movies
to invest in plywood futures

cuz the shop window
shows me the goods
just as it reflects my image
          back at my looking

          30% off.
          3.9 APR.
          19 loading bays.
          15 million dollars.
          405 arrests.
                    Four one five
                              Two eight five
                                        Ten eleven.

          & so tomorrow
                    I will join
                    the poets

    & the day after
          I will leave them

    & the day after that
          begins the clean up

          & the rethink
          & the revamp

& the day after that
& the night after that
& the day after that
& the night after that
& the day after that
& the night after that

DISTANCE NOW CLOSED BETWEEN

—Original Message—
From: OPD Operations
Sent: Tue 10/25/2011 12:58 PM
To: OPD Operations; Israel, Jeffrey; Allison, Darren; Poirier,
Michael; Santana, Deanna; Poulson, Edward; Parris, Kenneth;
Garcia, Gilbert; Whent, Sean; Wiley, Kevin; Rachal, Anthony; Davis,
Johnny; Lindsey, Drennon; Medeiros, Brian K.; Joyner, Ersie; Wong,
Clifford W; Mestas, Fred; Lozares, Demetrio; Tull, Steven; Hamilton,
Freddie; Williams, Sharon J; Shannon, Christopher; Outlaw,
Danielle; DL – OPD – Sergeants; Jordan, Howard; Breshears, Eric

Situation Update #15—Operation FOP 25 OCT 2011 @ 1254 hours

2nd/Washington parking enforcement being followed by protestors,
TNT responding. 14/bway 2 units responding here code 3, per
dispatch there is a 943 here. Per Cpt Joyner enough units here to
handle incident no need for more units. Patch Patrol 1/5 possibly
being surrounded here. One I/C at 14/bway. Patrol units are being
surrounded channel went code 33. Radio advised not to send any
more patrol units here let units respond with helmets. Bravo 91
channel can be unpatched @1256hrs

Situation Update #19—Operation FOP 25 OCT 2011 @ 1428 hours

Per Chief Jordan protestors have found out the Mayors address,
requesting units to be sent there to do a security check. Also giving
AC Transit updates regarding reroutes.

NOISE IN THE FACE OF

Now the shadow of the column—
as it stretches diagonally across

the square, the bronze figure falling
slowly, anti-newsreel'd or

slower still: a painting, a litho-
graph, to be printed and posted

on the boarded-up windows—
the shadow slicing clocks in two

divides the corresponding square:
dust-covered reds on one side,

on the other, the cops,
the emperor perched atop

his collapsing concrete mount,
glazed in bronzed afternoon

light, the moment between
the crash and the crowd's roar

an epic silent gap, film-stilled,
an historical engraving

upon the bodies of those
who roped and pulled

a millisecond-long victory
over art and anti-art both

nostalgia or history
or a painting of the same name

its first line from *A Project
for a Revolution in New*—

its last, Courbet:
"The essence of realism

is its negation of the ideal."
Thus the coins minted from

the smelted brass horses,
rubbed clean of their markings

by the partisans of negation,
for the image comes after—

even as it's ever always
in the present tense.

*

for the writing comes after—
debt—to what or whom,

scrivened on the column,
a tagger's quick retort:

now whose life's in pieces—
as the connoisseurs rush about

price-tagging each cold chip,
morgue'd for the toe-tagged index

as the television skycam snaps
tomorrow's front page pic—

in shards, remains, whatever,
the square a minefield peopled

by ghosts, by artists' models,
by narcs and turncoats greasy

the painter waits for tomorrow
's news, tagged to the grid—

point and click and dab and smear
and paste the concrete dust to bear

the weight of just-now's consequence
in some history painting's future frame

the square, rectangled, frenzy turned
to math, then scanned for hi-rez prints

while the handheld blocks of broken
concrete arc through gas-laced air,

ever hung there between
the photo and its subjects

until "you can hear the sirens
through the speaker-phones"

*

or words on the page, read,
in video art voice-over

at the museum of the riot
built with cobblestones and spit

like a youtube video
made with stolen gear

and unliked by everyone
til the algorithm splits itself

in two, one the true demo-
graphic, the other its shadow

falling across the spreadsheet
like a TED talk in reverse

the graphs and pie charts bleeding
as the smug smiles crossfade out

til all you see's the money
cultured in petrified design

pulsing earnings ratios and
quarterly arrest reports

pixels falling from the sky
ticker taped the market crash

onto those still stuck in
the plaza, or the painting, or

panting on the treadmill,
reading the liner notes

wiki'd to my sense of red
history, red scrims, re-read

threats to shut down the port,
the airport, the port-a-potty,

whatever it takes, like, what-
ever it takes to find a copy

of Jean Nuchtern's review
in the *Soho Weekly News*

of Rainer's anti-dance or since
I can't find that, why not,

Rainer Werner's unshot script
for *A Project for a Revolution*

starring, oh, I dunno, every-
body? all the gender-outlaws,

set to simmer, in exposition or
occupation or hotel lobby bars,

is that a gimlet or a knife,
a fake security pass or what

might pass for leaflets
in "an era of online doubt"

handing out the paper cuts
and a lifetime supply

of wheatpaste for all
that oozes beyond our means

to represent, to make anti-art
and unmake art, to shatter—

to rope and pull, to smash
the present, chalky with the dust

that never settles, noise
in the face of every apologist

for corporate lobby art,
high-concept design—budgeted

against the breaking point, of
sculpture, of plate glass, of friends

caked in pigpen grit, burnt doc-
ument scraps rising, shadowed

'gainst the columns of the fallen,
yet to be built, never to be but—

*

febrile pixelations, spec-
ulative reps, printers ink,

the scream that propels,
teaches, stretches, transmits

across "domains for going
astray," essaying athwart

the smashed column, riprap
for barricades, fodder for

a monograph on looking back,
the crowd in reverse, running

towards what it could become,
its power in that swell of

radiant expression, destructive,
how to have descriptivized it,

in oil paint, grease paint,
gas lines, water lines, figures,

it's "not just the cops—it's
the geometry"—kettled

mass ornament, mass canvass
stretched across the square

ash-can realism of the re-
hearsals for the water riot

and now in the face of
all that, all that is

the still-falling column, cropped
horses loosed from their owners'

leather-bound portfolios,
a cubist insurrection

demanding a counter-fit, go
fetch the spanners and let's—

DISTANCE NOW CLOSED BETWEEN

Situation Update #21—Operation FOP 25 OCT 2011 @ 1603 hours

Another 40 people towards the library, total of 200 people at the library. Will provide update every 5 mins.

Situation Update #23—Operation FOP 25 OCT 2011 @ 1614 hours

14/alice there is a march (80-100 people) headed eastbound in the middle of the street—also a group marching eastbound 14th, taking the street

Situation Update #25—Operation FOP 25 OCT 2011 @ 1620 hours

Crowd becoming big, starting to shut down traffic. 973 to post at all intersections north and south of 13th near the Library

HELLAGRAMS

HAVE YOU EVER SEEN A CROWD CHANGE ITS
COLLECTIVE MIND OR DON'T STOP DO A U TURN
WITHOUT A BULLHORN AT THE MOMENT OF DON'T
STOP SILENCE PHOTO OP CHRIS M SHOUTED
DON'T STOP I'M TIRED OF BEING SILENT I
WANT TO MAKE SOME FUCKING NOISE DON'T
STOP TWO NIGHTS EARLIER WE'D GOTTEN WORD
THAT ZIMMERMAN WOULD WALK RIGHT AS ALI
WAS GIVING HIS REPORT BACK FROM TURKEY
DON'T STOP AT THE HOLDOUT THE SMOKING
SECTION WAS SPLIT BETWEEN CYNICAL OF
COURSES AND LIP SNARLING DON'T STOP FURY
WHEN THE TALK WAS OVER J--- STOOD UP AND
SAID OGP AT 9 GO HOME DON'T STOP AND GET
YOUR TOOLS AND WITHIN A HALF HOUR IT WAS
DON'T STOP BIKES AND BEERS AND FLASKS AND
MASKS AND A BRISK CHILL IN THE AIR BUT A
CLEAR ENOUGH DON'T STOP NIGHT REQUIRING
NO BANNERS NO CAMERAS THE CROWD KNOWS IT-
SELF SOMEONE PROBABLY SAID DON'T STOP BY
ITS DECISIONS AND DEEDS HASHTAG SHIT AF-
FECT THEORY COULD LEARN FROM DON'T STOP

EVERYONE HAS THEIR OWN MJ STORY SO DON'T STOP HERE'S MINE IT'S THE NIGHT DON'T STOP BEFORE THE FIRST RAID AND THE GA'S DON'T STOP DEBATING HOW TO RESPOND TO THE EVICTION NOTICE AND CRAZY LADY DON'T STOP KEEPS SHOUTING WE LOVE YOU MICHAEL JACK-SON DON'T STOP UNTIL SOMEONE CALLS TIME OUT AND BLASTS DON'T STOP MJ FOR A TEN MINUTE DANCE BREAK SO THE GA COULD DON'T STOP WORK IT OUT AND THEN ONE TWO THREE DON'T STOP NIGHTS LATER WHEN THE VOTE CAME DOWN FOR THE STRIKE DON'T STOP RIGHT AT TEN WHEN OPD HAD THREATENED TO RAID AGAIN AND DON'T STOP OSF WAS CALLING FOR REINFORCEMENTS SINCE THEY WERE BEING RAIDED TOO DON'T STOP AND AS WE CHANTED STRIKE STRIKE STRIKE DON'T STOP SOMEONE PUT THRILLER ON AND SOME SPLIT DON'T STOP TO BART TO SF THOUGH THEY CLOSED THE DOWNTOWN STATION DON'T STOP TO PREVENT US STRIKE STRIKE STRIKE FROM GETTING THERE DON'T STOP WE ALL THREW DOWN TO MJ DON'T STOP STRIKE STRIKE STRIKE SINGING FTP FOR PYT DON'T STOP BECAUSE THE NIGHT BECAUSE THE DON'T STOP DOWNBEAT BEATDOWN BECAUSE THE THROWDOWNS TO COME DON'T STOP TIL YOU GET ENOUGH

THEN I THOUGHT DON'T STOP THAT IT'D BE
BEST TO DON'T STOP PUT IT ALL IN AND MAKE
IT A PLAY DON'T STOP THE STAGE DIRECTIONS
WOULD BE SIMPLE DON'T STOP ANYONE CAN
PLAY ANY PART IN FACT DON'T STOP IT
WOULDN'T BE PLAYING A PART BUT PLAYING
YOURSELF DON'T STOP MORE LIKE ANYONE
COULD SAY ANY LINE DON'T STOP AT ANY TIME
AS LONG AS DON'T STOP THE LINE KEPT MOV-
ING I MEAN DON'T STOP THE MARCH OR NOT A
MARCH BUT DON'T STOP THE ENSEMBLE THOUGH
THAT'S NOT THE RIGHT WORD WOULD DON'T
STOP SNAKE MARCH THROUGH DOWNTOWN DON'T
STOP OR THROUGH THE ART DON'T STOP MURMUR
AND THE LINES ARE FOR USING WHEN AND
DON'T STOP WHEREVER AND OF COURSE THE
MORE PLAYERS THE BETTER MAYBE DON'T STOP
THE SCRIPT WOULD BE CUT UP AND LINES
HANDED OUT OR NO DON'T STOP IT'S ON END-
LESS SHUFFLE ON THE SOUND SYSTEM DON'T
STOP BEING PUSHED THROUGH THE STREETS AND
DON'T STOP THERE ARE HELLA BULLHORNS THAT
CAN BE PASSED AROUND OR NO DON'T STOP
THERE SHOULDN'T BE A SCRIPT NO ONE NEEDS
DON'T STOP TO READ A PLAY CALLED SNAKE
MARCH MAYBE IT'S BETTER TO DON'T STOP
LEAVE IT ALL OUT AS LONG AS WE KEEP GOING
KEEP MOVING KEEP MAKING UP THE LINES AND
DON'T STOP

THEN WE WOULD SMASH DON'T STOP INTO THE
PIANO STORE AND ROLL DON'T STOP OUT A
BABY GRAND ON WHEELS DON'T STOP AND SET
IT ON FIRE WHILE PUSHING DON'T STOP IT UP
14TH TO BROADWAY AS SOMEBODY DON'T STOP
PLAYS THE VAMP TO THE COUP'S DON'T STOP
5000 WAYS TO DON'T STOP KILL A CEO THE
FLAMES FLARE DON'T STOP UP FROM THE
STRINGS AS THEY SNAP SOMEONE SINGS OUT
DON'T STOP KEEP ON PUSHIN KEEP ON PUSHIN
AND WHEN WE DON'T STOP HIT BROADWAY AND
THE LINE OF COPS DON'T STOP OUR INSTRU-
MENT BECOMES OUR SHIELD AND DON'T STOP
FROM THE PIANO BENCH SOMEONE PULLS DON'T
STOP A BAG OF BALL BEARINGS WHICH THEY
FLING DON'T STOP AT THE FEET OF THE COPS
AND I PLAY DON'T STOP THE BENNY HILL
THEME SONG AND WE ALL DON'T STOP HIT THE
DECK SNAP CRACKLE DON'T STOP

AT THE GA BEFORE THE MARCH TEARDROP ASKED
WHAT DID A WINDOW EVER DO TO YOU AND
SOMEONE YELLED DON'T STOP IT KEEPS ME
FROM THEIR MONEY AND SOMEONE YELLED IT
KEEPS ME FROM THE SHIT I NEED BUT DON'T
STOP THAT NIGHT THERE WAS NO SOUND SYSTEM
AND THAT DON'T STOP MORE THAN THE SILENCE
OF UNBROKEN GLASS MADE US WANT TO DON'T
STOP SCREAM AT THE PRESS TRAILING IN
DROVES HOPING FOR SOME RIOT DON'T STOP
PORN ONE YEAR SINCE THE FIRST RAID AND
THE AFTERGAS POLITICAL FAIL BLOG TOLD ME
DON'T STOP HE HAD OPEN QUOTES TALKED TO
THE BLACK BLOC CLOSE QUOTES AND WE WERE
LIKE WTF BUT HE SAID NO DON'T STOP SMASHY
AND ALL I COULD THINK ABOUT WAS DON'T
STOP THE PLANNING GROUP AND HOW WE FUCKED
UP DON'T STOP BY NOT BOTTOMLINING A SOUND
SYSTEM WHILE THE WORD WENT AROUND DON'T
STOP THAT THOSE OF US ARRESTED ON 025
LAST YEAR MIGHT DON'T STOP STILL HAVE
THEIR CHARGES BROUGHT BEFORE THE DEADLINE
PASSED DON'T STOP AND THEN JAIL YOU FOR
CONTEMPT IF YOU DON'T DON'T STOP CHECK
YOUR MAIL AND SHOW UP LIKE TOMORROW OR
WAS IT TOMORROW ALREADY DON'T STOP WE'D
BEEN MARCHING ALL NIGHT

WE READ THAT IF BEING DASH WITH IS THE
SHARING DON'T STOP OF A SIMULTANEOUS
SPACE DASH TIME THEN DON'T STOP IT IN-
VOLVES A PRESENTATION OF THIS SPACE DASH
TIME AS SUCH DON'T STOP IN ORDER TO SAY
WE ONE MUST PRESENT THE HERE DON'T STOP
AND NOW OF THIS WE DON'T STOP WE CAN
NEVER SIMPLY BE A WE DON'T STOP UNDER-
STOOD AS A UNIQUE SUBJECT DON'T STOP WE
ALWAYS EXPRESSES A PLURALITY DON'T STOP
EXPRESSES OUR BEING DON'T STOP DIVIDED
AND ENTANGLED DON'T STOP

THEN I THOUGHT DON'T STOP I'D CONSTRUCT
AN ELABORATE POEM DON'T STOP BASED ON AN
ACAB RHYME DON'T STOP SCHEME OR N PLUS
SEVEN DON'T STOP IT ALL COPULAS ARE
BATHROBES DON'T STOP IN ORDER TO HAVE THE
DON'T STOP FORM EXPRESS THE POLITICS
DON'T STOP DIRECTLY PLUS IT'D BE HELLA
CLEVER BUT DON'T STOP EVERYONE KNOWS ALL
CATS ARE BEAUTIFUL DON'T STOP AND THE
REST JUST FELT MORE LIKE FILL DON'T STOP
IN THE BLANKS OR SHOOTING DON'T STOP
BLANKS AND NOT FT POPO DON'T STOP THEN
CHRIS AND MELVIN AND DON'T STOP LADY GAGA
AND THE TACTICAL ACTION CREW SHOWED UP
DON'T STOP WITH A FOUR LANE WIDE FTP BAN-
NER SCREAMING DON'T STOP TO THE PIGPEN
AND IT WAS ALL DON'T STOP CONTENT COMMA
MEET FORM COMMA MEET SATURDAY NIGHT DON'T
STOP TIL THE NEW YEAR BLEW UP

THOSE OF US WHO DIDN'T GET DON'T STOP
SNATCHED MADE IT TO RADIO FOR WHISKEYS
AND BEERS AND OMGS DON'T STOP BILL WAS
WALKING AROUND POPPING DON'T STOP
ACUPUNCTURE STUDS INTO OUR EARS TO TAME
THE DON'T STOP ADRENALINE AS SOMEONE
PULLED UP A PHOTO OF DEREK DON'T STOP
SMILING INSIDE CITY HALL AS THE FLAG
BURNED IT WAS ALREADY POSTED ON USA DON'T
STOP TODAY DOT COM LESS THAN AN HOUR
AFTER WE'D RUN DON'T STOP ACROSS OGP AN-
NOUNCING THAT CITY HALL WAS NOW OPEN
DON'T STOP FOR MONKEY BIDNESS AND LESS
THAN AN HOUR SINCE DON'T STOP STAY CALM
DON'T PANIC DON'T STOP AND WHAT SIX SEVEN
FOUR NINE HOURS SINCE THE BEANBAG WHIZZED
BY OUR EARS OUTSIDE THE MUSEUM DON'T STOP
AND KALAMITY CAME TO THE DOOR SHOUTING
DON'T STOP THEY'RE DRIVING UP AND DOWN
THE STREETS IN VANS SNATCHING PEOPLE AND
WE WONDERED IF THERE WAS A BACK DOOR OR
IF WE DON'T STOP WERE TRAPPED INSIDE IF
AND WHEN THE COPS DON'T STOP SINCE THEY
KNEW WHERE WE DRANK AND PROBABLY DON'T
STOP HAD BUGGED THE CAGED SMOKE ROOM UP-
STAIRS BUT DON'T STOP THEN THE DJ PUT ON
RIHANNA AND WE BOUNCED UP AND DOWN DON'T
STOP BOUNCING UP AND DOWN DON'T STOP IN
THE NAME OF LULZ

DISTANCE NOW CLOSED BETWEEN

Situation Update #27—Operation FOP 25 OCT 2011 @ 1627 hours

Everything is locked down on 14th st. No traffic coming from East Oakland along 14th st twds downtown. 15th st/Madison is where the hole is, this is where the traffic is. 17/Madison has stopped all south bound traffic.

Situation Update #28—Operation FOP 25 OCT 2011 @ 1700 hours

Crowd abt 600, 4-5 people masking up. 50-60 people on bikes. Snow Park is clear. Argus will be up in a minute or so. Bart is still up and running

Situation Update #30—Operation FOP 25 OCT 2011 @ 1736 hours

Lead of crowd w/b Webster. Santa Clara to stage inside of PAB. Argus advising not enough units at Webster. Will have police presence near the freeway entrance. Traffic needs to be stopped S/B 14th. Crowd is cooperative. 8 Motors ert to enforce @ 12/bway. 12/Bway overtaken.

WE FOUND LULZ IN A HAPLESS PLACE

                              does form make demands?

wait, what?

        to "make gestures quotable"

                the better business bureau asks.

An Oakland poet in San Francisco.
A San Francisco poet in Oakland.

        "(or indeed the police force, in current procedurals

Owns a stapler gun.

                ("comes into its own
                        mode of representation

accounting
    vs.
recounting

<swipe>

                ("it is rather   bureaucracy
                        whose   epic is sung
                        before us")

An actual explosion, in an actual shingle factory.

in 1913.
in 1934.

but that's not my File
Transfer Protocol

would you prefer a reference
to Shelley here?

or to the licorice strike?

"ATTICA! ATTICA!"   "ATTICA! ATTICA!"

screams Al Pacino, in a Raiders jacket.

but: "The image is always in the present tense."

A group of rich people, caring about the environment.

to get to the other side.

the synopticon asks.

An Oakland poet in Santa Cruz.
An Oakland poet in Davis.

problem: articulating an us
that makes we happen
beyond us-ies.
thus

the where of we
   vs.
the when of we

      and: that one guy who won't shut up.

to describe
the "gesture
of falling silent"

      of heads down on the sidelines

    of neck bent into the screen-feed

        of looking over one's shoulder

      to talk behind one's own back

Problem: "the possibility of communal speech (poetry) in the absence of a 'we.'"

but: —"we
         —there is no 'we'
         —let us separate ourselves now"

        and: our capacitors, their selves

          so: affect looks like what—?

    to fetch some aluminum bats.

a re-enactment of the Battle of Oak Street.

    in 1946.
    in 2013.
         wait, what?

what rhetorics of temporality to describe—'it'
                                    its having been

         "tighten up! tighten up!"

     the view from above asks.

A New York poet in Oakland.
An Oakland poet in Danville.

Youth
   vs.
"the youth"

      <swipe>

"WOUNDED KNEE! WOUNDED KNEE!"
                "WOUNDED KNEE! WOUNDED KNEE!"

      screams Little Joe Killsright,
            through a black and red bandana.

"and then I became—
         and this is in Vegas—
         okay, this is an arrow—
         right now, this is me, see ...   but I don't think about,
               y'know, taking up
            a revised Rihanna song, y'know, heh—she
               basically latched on—
"(youtube, Michelle, get fit, all the kids, and so)"
            ...to what happens in certain communities"
"(diseases, obesity, see what I'm sayin', there's no thought,
      no job, and so   I need)"

                        had to financialize the climate
                        in order to save it

40

"and then I got board certified"

Problem: emotion recollected in tranquility. Fuck tranquility.
        but: ordering a Jameson with a single ice cube.
                        Recollecting that.

        to concretize disgust.   as a positive
                           way of saying
                                No.

              the certifying board asks.

An Oakland poet in Vancouver.
An Oakland poet in Kansas City.

        in 1985.
        in 2014.

              A group of rich people, foraging in a forest.

100 fire extinguishers, aimed at the approaching line.

                    Beyond the kettle,
                    another kettle,
                    called work.

                    Hedging debt
                    on the no-futures
                    market.

such that: All Drones Are Zimmerman.

But not only are my desires not being met, they're not
        even my desires.

Learning from Las Vegas
   vs.
Learning from Lagos

     in 1977.
     in 2006.

          would you like a reference
          to Koolhaus here?

          or to the defense of the RCA?

"But plausible deniability is itself
an architectural choice, one made manifest
not only in procurements and mergers,
not only in networks and protocols,
but also in drywall and concrete and stock photography."

        Tho some bodies
        are forgotten
        in the language
        compound—

Problem: who's not in the photo?

<swipe>

cuz they're tools, questions are

"the Arab Street thinks"
   vs.
"the Oakland Street thinks"

Last night the DJ fueled our fight
& today, hazy & blasted
hustling for the bail fund

>   red and black laughter
>   red and black nights

>   But how does it make you feel?

>   the morning after.
>   at $160 an hour.

>   <swipe>

"a pedagogy of space and time"
    vs.
the state and the clock

>   but structures
>   don't take
>   to the street
>   , cuz

>   when you're pushing the sound
>   system up the street
>   in SF you gotta
>   watch for the tracks

>   & give up yr umbrella
>   to cover the battery
>   as the rain falls
>   on Wall Street West

>   in advance of the pepper spray
>   cuz when the skirmish

line's out front
others can sneak

in the back & banner drop
which is when you want
the speakers to kick
& the mic to crackle

the call for medics
to help wash out the eyes
of all who can't see
the paint on the walls:

Run comrade
the old world's
behind you

"That night I/we pulled out a piece of paper and started writing, well, of course—we had just stimulated each other, had just put ideas first, had just created a void we were all dying to fill! The desire to make something, to solve what was stumping—all this came from "we". Desire. So yes, I ... did the actual writing ... but desire came with the 'we'."

experiments in representation
the "syntax of fighting to actually win"

A group of rich people, cleaning
a swimming pool.

<swipe>

and: who counts what, by what metrics.
beyond the clicks, the "slowly fading pings..."

a series
of data
packets

constitutes
a set trans-
versing

the field,
spreadsheets
on the grass,

alas, pigeon
shit occludes
the equation

no work today
so get to it

        and by won one means owned

  "RUBY RIDGE! RUBY RIDGE!"
        RUBY RIDGE! RUBY RIDGE!"

     screams Steve Kurtz, through
        a Lackawanna surgical mask

   and: better meetings.

          wait, what?

Watching
a video
of Lumumba

on a phone
made of Congolese
colton

                                    face paint selfie
                                    phone swiping technology

(uptalked:)
"I think it opens the door to bringing counter-
                              surveillance into fashion?"

                    to capture the hot new look on the street.

                         the feds ask.

A Ugandan poet in Vancouver.
A black bloc poet at the MLA.

                    When is "I"? When are "she"? When is "we"?

That guy? He's his own tendency.

Broadside fetishist.

Backstabber.

Hand-wringer.

Online commenter.

46

Problem: what I heard was image-captured off your
feed in response to that other thing ppl were talking
about, and that being considered politics.

    and: it is. even if I'd rather etc.,

        yet: "we need toilets and a kitchen"

    A group of rich people, each with their own
    personal philosophies.

"FERGUSON! FERGUSON!"
        "FERGUSON! FERGUSON!"

    screams Lil' Bobbie Hutton, buried in a hoodie

But how does it make you *think*?

    To bottom-line the booze run.

        The multitude (of seven) asks.

An Oakland poet in Philly.
A rich poet in Oakland.

    then
    soon we'll have
    a 3D printer

    for all the tools
    we need for nights
        like this

now what, wait?

But how does it make you *smell?*

the % of Silicon Valley janitors living in Oakland
    vs.
the % of Oakland cops living outside of Oakland

"tighten up! tighten up!"

would you like a reference
to Angela Davis here?

or to Freedom TV Nyamubaya?

"Envy those meetings? Good.
As a feminist I want you to drool for such a 'we'."

in 1982.
in 2015.

Problem: sick of poetry, not finding another form
    for this roving disgust.

Like escaping a fire in a building that you designed.
    while hating metaphors   and prosody
then running back in, to log back on and

<swipe>

yet: those stabbing keyboard triplets.
    the oh shit here it comes.

"tighten up! tighten up!"

in & across the intersection

whose we to act
as if of us

    so remember
    to carry
    your meds

    in their original
    labeled
    bottles

    in case
    you get
    snatched

      wait, what—who's we? whose?

        Everyone in the street
            is in this fucking dance—

        now pick up a tool
        and fucking garden.

DISTANCE NOW CLOSED BETWEEN

Situation Update #31—- Operation FOP 25 OCT 2011 @ 1757 hours

7/Bway blking traffic. All mobile field force relocating here. CHP sending 2 squads to ramps of freeway. Also broadcasted info regarding vigil in area of 18/mlk at the Church for 187 victim. Crowd headed westbound. Gilroy motors being sent to 8th/Bwy. Line held at 8th/bwy to make an arrest. Crowd headed w/b 7th street now. Per Argus officer is surrounded at 7th/Washington.

Situation Update #32—- Operation FOP 25 OCT 2011 @ 1804 hours

7th/Washington was code 33 per Argus uncooperative protestors. Gas was deployed here also. Unit calling unlawful assembly. 7th/Clay appears to be peaceful. 8th/Clay protestors masking up. 7th/Washington unites will be forming a Scirmish Line. Hostiles are at 8th/Washington per Argus. Making 3rd announcement for unlawful assembly. Large group frm Washington/8th st

WE DO THE POLIS

How to make
nothing happen

until there's
something

there in that
negation

where we want
to have begun

Of space-time
compression

momentum
without target

running not
yet amok

inside the tent-
ative present.

Of duration
scansion'd into

communiqués
disguised as poems

in whatever
time this is

here on the
trampled grass

We are not
permitted

to return
to a meadow

tho often
we do

it's a ban-
ner night

In the epic
gap that splits

actors from
their lines

the play-
ing field

opens ops
for now-times

Crisis-time
makes its own sun

"brushstrokes
before action"

leave the banners
bring the noise

then shoot out
the fucking clocks

Pent up
in a narrow

compass
and shortened

on every side
by the neigh-

borhood
of walls

These veterans
of future wars

handing out
the PTSD

brieflets before
having been

vowel'd-out
gears & wrenches

Thus striking,
verbing, swerved

and swayed
into sieves

maneuvering
toward

fissures
in the line

Swallowed
the scare quotes

and choked on
what hung

in the air
around me

stripped of that
security

A field
of intensities

that pulse
through a set

of others
coaligned

in throng
song

What poetry
is this

happening
too fast

to count
the syllables

in each throat's
retort

In the photo
I'm dancing

and the photo's
on the internet

geo-tagged
to the night

we swayed again-
st the sound

Even as
we knew

it would
never last

long enough
for this to

have become
an epic poem

Fences
down

kitchens
up

it's what
we call

adaptive
design

Like using
a hammer

to make
an ATM

from a park-
ing meter.

Crack it
open, cuz

Police realism
bounds in

to contain
the crowd

squeeze
the schema

til it pops
and unlocks

Uneven
development

uneven
poetics

we were
the crisis

now we're
the consequence

The improbable
trembles

in each arched
body

what are
the forms

we'd like
to live in

From I to
we is an other

zoned outside
coterie comforts

the forms
drop away

and new ones
rise up

DISTANCE NOW CLOSED BETWEEN

Situation Update #34—- Operation FOP 25 OCT 2011 @ 1838 hours

Public works has pulled out of the plaza. Crowd moving northbound
Bwy. Per Argus very little movement of crowd. 50-100 protestors
starting to moving northbound Bwy. Group sitting down at 14/bwy.
2 Sheriff buses en route. Chp H30 taking over for Argus while they
refuel. Per Argus 800-1000 protestors southbound 19/bwy. Tail of
crowd at San Pablo. Holding now at 1700 Bwy taking over the street
stopping traffic.

Situation Update #36—- Operation FOP 25 OCT 2011 @ 1920 hours

Argus back on scene at Snow Park. Restablished barriers around
the plaza. If anyone takes them down they are arrestable. Crowd is
clearing Harrison approaching Webster. Crowd has grown 1200-
1400 protestors at 20/bwy.

EVERYTHING IS PIXELATED

1. Instructions For a Dance I Refuse to Perform

Stand center stage, facing those who are looking at you. First, raise your right elbow out to the right, at ninety-degrees from your side. Now move your forearm up from your elbow at a forty-five-degree angle, twist your wrist and hold your hand straight in front of your forehead. Hold this for two seconds and then drop your arm, putting both hands in your pockets.

Now slowly walk backwards, first the right foot and then the left. Look at those in front of you who are looking at you. Stop and lean forward with your upper torso, keeping your lower body in alignment with your spine, and then straighten back up and take four quick small steps backwards. Take your hands out of your pockets and do this again.

Use your calf muscles to keep you balanced as you lean forward. Then take four quick small steps backwards, then two steps forward, then eight steps back. Stop and touch your right hand to the right side of your mouth and drop it down again. Now turn to your right, using your left shoulder to pull your upper torso in that direction, which in turn pulls the lower half of your body with it as you twist at the waist.

Bend both arms at the elbows until your wrists are just above your waist and then sashay sideways to your right. Shuffle around the stage, your left foot hitting the inside of the right, which then skips out to the side, etc. Raise your left arm up and down as you do this, and then bend your right knee outwards and to the side. Engage your oblique muscles to pull your body inward and down. Curl your right elbow and shoulder forward and kick your left leg out to the side until you are lying on your right side. From this position, contract your abdominal muscles and use this flexion to pull your left elbow and left knee together.

Stay in this position for five seconds.

Now stand and raise both your arms in front of you until they are parallel to the ground. Put your weight onto your left foot and lift your right leg up, bent at the knee. Straighten your left arm and reach down as if about to touch the ground. Then swiftly flex your abdominal muscles inward, pulling your upper torso downward. Bend your left leg and raise your right arm up. Hop once backwards as you fall onto your ass.

Roll onto your left side. Press your left shoulder, ribs, and hip against the ground. Raise your right leg and bend it at a 45-degree angle, while raising your right arm and doing the same. Shift back and forth on the ground for six seconds. Move your body to the left and to the right as your abdominal muscles flex and release, pulling you up and then back down.

Now stand and turn perpendicular to those who are watching you. Raise your left arm out to your side and then do the same with your right arm, keeping this arm bent at the elbow. Now shuffle forward and back, waving your left arm up and down slightly. Keep your wrist loose and fingers spread slightly open. Take one step forward and then two steps back. Sashay away from those who are watching you.

Now take five steps across the stage from left to right and then pause, swaying in place from right to left. Then, using your spine as an axis and your knees as support, rapidly turn clockwise 270 degrees to the right and drop yourself to the ground, twisting as you do this until you are flat on your back. Keep in mind that your organs will shift in response to the sudden movement. Contract your abdominal and psoas muscles in order to force the air out of your lungs. Take a large breath in and then repeat the forced exhalation.

Maintaining the contact of your back to the ground, rotate your body 180 degrees clockwise. Look straight up at the ceiling or sky. Continue to breathe in the forced manner of before. Engage the intercostal muscles beneath your ribs to push your lungs in and out. Now spin your body around again, your back pressed to the ground, one and a half full rotations counter-clockwise, for a total of 540 degrees. Wait a beat and then allow your shoulder and upper torso muscles to lift you up. Let your head hang slack as you rise to your feet.

Now face forward again. Open and close your mouth three times while bending your right arm in front of you and thrusting it up and down at those who are watching you. Shift your weight to the right, then rotate your torso at the waist in that direction. Hold your right arm up and bend the forearm back at the elbow until it is chin-high and horizontal. Then jerk back to your left. Now fall quickly onto your right side, then roll to the left onto your back, with your arms bent up at the elbows and hands slack.

Using your hamstrings and upper back muscles, shift your entire body two inches to the left in one movement. Now lift your right arm and throw it over your body to the left. Kick your right leg over the left, using all your strength to throw yourself over onto your front. When you land your feet should be slightly spread, your right arm out in front of you, your head turned to the left and resting on your bent left arm. Now clench your neck muscles and jerk your head off your forearm and to the right. Twist your right arm behind your back until your wrist is touching your belt. Squeeze your shoulder blades toward each other and feel your stomach muscles clenching.

Now repeat that last part again, just the flip from your back to your front. Again, begin by thrusting your right arm over your torso and kicking your right leg over the left, thus pulling the rest of your body up and over until you land face down. Try to do so in a way that will lift you off the ground during the flip. Don't just roll over. Let your body flip.

Do it again.

Again.

Now repeat this one more time, but as slowly as possible. Try to use every muscle in your body to lift yourself off the ground and flip over onto your front, your head turned to the left and resting on your bent left arm, your legs straight out and slightly spread. Clench your neck muscles and slowly pull your head off your left arm and to the right. Internally rotate your right arm 180 degrees in its socket and then flex the elbow back, adducting it towards your midline. Now slowly squeeze your shoulder blades towards each other and feel your stomach muscles clenching. Twist your right wrist up and to the left. Rotate your left arm in its socket and bend it at the elbow. Your pectoral and lateral muscles will need to stretch as you twist your left wrist up and over to your spine. Now stay perfectly still, holding this position until further instructions.

2. Riot Porn Power Point

[slide]

He will begin by standing center stage, in front of a dark screen, his feet planted about shoulder-width apart, his arms at his sides, his gaze soft and aimed in the general direction of the audience but without any clear focus or eye contact. He will likely be nervous, more or less depending on whatever demographic he imagines is constituted in the audience, his hands might be sweaty, his heart might be beating faster than usual. All of these affective states, however, will remain interior and ideally invisible to viewers.

To the side of the stage his collaborator will stand facing him from stage left and then begin to read the performance score. The reading will be directed at him, the score functioning as a set of instructions for him to follow. The instructions are for different ways to move his body, and are mostly simple and somewhat banal.

[slide]

Rather than following the instructions, however, he will continue standing still, his legs spread shoulder-width apart, his arms at his side save for the occasional nose-scratch or minor fidgeting, and throughout the presentation of the movement score he will resist following it. Instead, audience members will see a white cis-male body standing more or less still on stage, listening to a set of increasingly abstract instructions for somewhat unconventional (though decidedly not 'dancerly') movements.

What the audience will not know at this point is that the performance score is designed for re-enactments of recent violent encounters with Bay Area riot cops. The instructions are based on the detailed movements of various bodies and body parts of protestors being beaten, appropriated from various livestream videos of protests and police riots. Given the graphic intensity of the images and the seeming immediacy of the relatively new documentary (and often narrated) practice of livestreaming, some have begun to speak of 'riot porn' as the name of an emergent genre and affective 'viewing experience.'

Whether used by activists to document police aggression and/or celebrate certain modes of resistance, or used by forces of reaction to justify predetermined narratives of 'unlawful' rebellion, the spread of so-called riot porn in the wake of recent insurrectionary movements around the globe and the increasingly reliance on social media for 'immediate' distribution have brought new questions about representations of violence to the fore.

[slide]

However, rather than perform the score, he will refuse to (even as the movement instructions continue to be read aloud, directed at him alone), in an attempt to foreground the limitations of re-enactment and performance to represent such scenes. Needless to say, when stripped down into linguistic instructions for movement, what would otherwise appear to be notations for nonrepresentational dance push against the 'loaded' source material, even if the content will have yet to be revealed to the audience. Meanwhile, spectators will continue to see a white cis-male body, removed from any risk of violence (though 'having been there,' whatever that might mean [which is very little, he thinks]), trying to represent the inability to fully represent something both embodied and spectacular, something that once aestheticized can take on elements of abstract contemporary dance as much as a 'realist' documentation of physical violence and repression.

Meanwhile, as the instructions continue to be read, he will think about what it means to refuse to re-enact certain content, while also staging that refusal, putting his body on display even as it can not possibly stand in for those bodes that he might wish to represent. How refusal itself can so easily become spectacularized, aestheticized, an empty gesture, especially if one has the privilege to choose refusal. He will nonetheless continue to stand and listen while his collaborator continues to read the score, feeling his body actively resist the temptation to follow the instructions, such that even as his 'refusal' demands only his non-compliance and thus should be incredibly easy to perform, his muscles nonetheless make minor movements, synapses firing within his sympathetic nervous system, and he will no doubt experience complex and fraught emotions neither explicit or implied in the choreographic score.

And perhaps he will be fretting over the audience's reaction to his passivity, his refusal, worrying about the presumed expectations of viewers of performance art or poetry, of what a performing body can or should do, of what constitutes something exciting, new, or merely 'interesting'. He might continue to indulge his anxiety by worrying that he should aim to entertain, to make an audience nod their heads in recognition or enjoyment, or alternatively gesture more explicitly towards recognizable political tropes, so that the 'seriousness' of the content is matched by the intensity of his affect, be it of righteous indignation or some kind of solidarity and fortitude. And all the while audience members will continue to watch a white cis-male standing more or less still on stage, listening along to a set of cues that he for some reason does not follow, perhaps drifting off in their boredom, tuning out the words that very well may sound more like ambient language than anything in relation to actual bodies and body parts moving in certain ways against their will, not in response to some choreographic score but forced by the tools of the militarized state exercising its own perverse performance of power through costumed and weaponized bodies.

[slide]

And perhaps during all of this he will be wearing all black, masked up with a vinegar-soaked bandana for visual and olfactory effect, suggesting a different kind of white cis-male body, both anonymous and yet over-determinedly public and 'militant', suggestive of certain actions and attitudes in the context of street battles with the cops. But more likely he will not, choosing to avoid any overtly referential or suggestive costuming or eye-rollingly self-aggrandizing props.

Or perhaps he will slowly remove his clothing, revealing bruises and welts on his body, marks that will have been the result of re-enacted beatings, having come into intimate relations with those collaborators willing to beat him—'for the sake of performance art,' he would embarrassingly plead—bruises he will have had to have produced in order to reproduce some kind of pseudo-realism, a kind of public solidarity with beaten comrades as well as an attempt to express some notion of fidelity to an increasingly celebrated ethos of re-enactment itself, wherein authenticity is taken for the ethical in and of itself, as if embodied mimesis were enough to effectively transmit political content. But no, he will keep his clothes on, as porn is not about nakedness, nor is the vulnerability of the performer (not to mention the incredibly clichéd and often narcissistic image of the masochistic straight white cis-male performance artist) the central concern here. And all the while the audience will continue looking (or looking away, in boredom or eye-rolling contempt) at a white cis-male standing still on stage, listening (or ignoring, out of boredom or tuned-out dismissal) to a set of banal instructions for some sort of imaginary dance performance.

[slide]

Finally, the instructions will cease. The lights will go down and the screen will light up. Finally, he will move, if only to get out of the way of the projector's pixelated beam. Finally, we will get to be proper spectators, with 'something to look at'. Finally, we will get to see the riot porn promised by the title. Finally, we will get to see the source material for the movement score he will have refused to re-enact. Yet during the scenes on screen he will repeat the score, as if presenting the instructions to the bodies we will see flailing on screen, their right arms flung out to the right or their left legs kicking out and up, their abdominal muscles contracting, their asses landing hard upon the concrete, until the disconnect between language and image, between spectatorship and voyeurism, between solidarity and appropriation, between re-enactment and its limitations, between political rage and artistic failure, between violence and its representation, between bodies and pixels, might find adequate expression in enacting one's refusal while still refusing not to act.

[slide]

3. Now Streaming Live

We watch you raise your right elbow out to the right, at ninety-degrees from your side. We watch you move your forearm up at a forty-five-degree angle at your elbow, holding your hand straight in front of your forehead, saluting the line of riot cops. We watch you hold this for two seconds and then drop your arm, putting both hands in your pockets.

Then we watch you slowly walk backwards, first the right foot and then the left. You stop and lean forward with your upper torso, keeping your lower body in alignment with your spine, and then straighten back up and take four quick small steps backwards. We watch you take your hands out of your pockets and do this again.

We watch you take four quick small steps backwards, then two steps forward, then eight steps back. We watch you stop and touch your right hand to the right side of your mouth and drop it down again. We watch you turn to your right, using your left shoulder to pull your upper torso in that direction, which in turn pulled the lower half of your body with it as you twisted at the waist.

We watch you bend both arms at the elbows until your wrists are just above your waist and then you sashay sideways to your right. We watch you shuffle around, your left foot hitting the inside of the right, which then skips out to the side. We watch you raise your left arm up and down as you do this, and then bend your right knee outwards and to the side. We watch you curl your right elbow and shoulder forward and kick your left leg out to the side until you are lying on your right side. We then watch you contract your abdominal muscles and use this flexion to pull your left elbow and left knee together. We watch as you stay in this position for five seconds, as one riot cop hits you with his baton and another kicks you.

We watch how you then stand and raise both your arms in front of you until they are parallel to the ground. How you put your weight onto your left foot and lift your right leg up, bent at the knee. We watch you straighten your left arm and reach down as if about to touch the ground. Then we watch as you swiftly flex your abdominal muscles inward, pulling your upper torso downward. We see you bend your left leg and raise your right arm up to block the blows of the baton. We watch how you hop once backwards and then fall onto your ass.

Then we watch you roll onto your left side and raise your right leg and bend it at a 45-degree angle, while raising your right arm and doing the same. We see you shift back and forth on the ground for six seconds. We watch you move your body to the left and to the right as your abdominal muscles flex and release, pulling you up and then back down.

Then we watch you stand and turn perpendicular to 'the viewers at home' as you raise your left arm out to your side and then we see you do the same with your right arm, keeping this arm bent at the elbow. Then we watch you shuffle forward and back, waving your left arm up and down slightly. We see how your wrist is loose and fingers spread slightly open. How you take one step forward and then two steps back. How you sashay away from those who watched safely from home.

We watch you take five steps from left to right and then pause, swaying in place from right to left. Then we watch you using your spine as an axis and your knees as support in order to rapidly turn clockwise 270 degrees to the right and drop yourself to the ground, twisting as you did this until you are flat on your back. We imagine you feeling your organs shift in response to the sudden movement.

As you are maintaining the contact of your back to the ground, we watch as you then rotate your body 180 degrees clockwise. We watch you look straight up at the sky. We see how you breathe in the forced manner of before. Next we watch as you spin your body around again, your back pressed to the ground, one and a half full rotations counter-clockwise, for a total of 540 degrees. After a beat we see the cop grab you by the arm to yank you up. We see how you let your head hang slack as you rise to your feet.

Then you are facing forward again. We watch you open and close your mouth three times while bending your right arm in front of you and thrusting it up and down at those watching. We watch you shift your weight to the right, then rotate your torso at the waist in that direction. Then we can see how you hold your right arm up and bend the forearm back at the elbow until it is chin-high and horizontal. Then we watch as you are jerked back to your left and then fall quickly onto your right side, then roll to the left onto your back, with your arms bent up at the elbows and hands slack.

We watch as your entire body is shifted two inches to the left in one movement. We watch as your right arm is lifted and thrown over your body to the left. We are looking at how you kick your right leg over the left, as you are thrown over onto your front. We can see how when you land your feet are slightly spread, your right arm out in front of you, your head turned to the left and resting on your bent left arm. Then we watch you clench your neck muscles as your head is jerked off your forearm and to the right. We see how your right arm is twisted behind your back until your wrist is touching your belt. It appears to us that you are then forced to squeeze your shoulder blades toward each other.

And now we watch that last part repeat, just the flip from your back to your front. Again, as your right arm is yanked over your torso, forcing you to kick your right leg over the left, thus pulling the rest of your body up and over until you land face down. We watch them do this to you in a way that lifts you off the ground during the flip. We watch it again. And then another time.

And then we watch this repeated one more time, but in slow-motion, the image clearly manipulated after the event, as if to help us see with more precision, outside the lived time of your experience. We look at the screen and watch as you are spun in the air, your head turned to the left and landing on your bent left arm, your legs straight out and slightly spread. We can see you clench your neck muscles and slowly pull your head off your left arm and to the right. We make sense of the projected images to understand how you are then forced to internally rotate your right arm 180 degrees in its socket and then your elbow is pulled back, adducting it towards your midline. Now we watch as you slowly squeeze your shoulder blades towards each other as your right wrist is twisted up and to the left. We can see now, viewing the video projection, how you are forced to also rotate your left arm in its socket and bend it at the elbow. We have seen this several times now. By looking at light projected onto a screen hung from the ceiling of a performance space, we can see how this is done against your will. We watch the cop press his knee into your back and cuff you. We watch you staying perfectly still, holding this position—against your will, regardless of ours—until the image fades into pixels and dust.

DISTANCE NOW CLOSED BETWEEN

Situation Update #37—- Operation FOP 25 OCT 2011 @ 1941 hours

Will allow protestors to peacefully protest. Not allowed to enter
Frank Ogawa plaza if so they are arrestable. Crowd at 1500 Bwy
holding. All units masking up making announcements at 14/Bwy
given 5 mins to leave area apx 1500-1700 protestors here. Crown
approaching barriers. Protestors have set up barriers, there is a bout
a 7ft gap between their barriers and ours. Something being broken
in the crowd, no visual. Distance now closed between barricades.
Now throwing objects. Gas being deployed into crowd.

Situation Update #38—- Operation FOP 25 OCT 2011 @ 2016 hours

Numerous tweets that the Occupy Oakland General Assembly
announced will meet everyday at 1800 hrs at 14th and Broadway
(info via Sgt Dinh, T.) Male mid eastern on a red yamaha F-4 street
bike w/ Camoflauge backpack handing out items to protestors in
crowd. Trash cans being set on fire at 14/bwy. Protestor in crowd
seen w/ a full triple CS de canister, suspect has wen back into the
crowd. Holmgren advising bag w/ canister was recovered. Crowd
now moving s/b San Pablo frm 20th. Argus down for fuel again,
H30 (CHO) taking over.

A SWARMING, A WOLFING

Perhaps then we will
might yet have become
scavengers of the unknown,
liberating the contact zones
where we find ourselves,
"lumpy and contestable
aggregates," that sweaty
and angered entanglement
of overripe species-beings
buzzing and dew-drunk
in the counter-future,
impure yet interdependent,
exercising significant otherness
in the shared scrum of bio-
political fleshwork and re-art-
iculatory speech actions,
forging new next-nows
in the microbial commons
of our shared social breath.

Went back to the plaza
and all I got were
these linked cuffs
but then what's the point
of an authorized protest.
It's like perfume. Gas.
But the glitter bloc's
got my back, up
against the forward heave
a free-for-all fire-drill
so let's meme out and
tear through the fences

                    The occupy poets brigade
          emergency
          group text service
          is now opera
                    -ational

Text back: what hpng? Poetry?

                              J: not sure where
                              Jack: on foot?

Am by the ice cream truck

Can you bounce
up and down?
So I can find you

J: Irene hit w canister

                         The page you are
                              viewing was en
                                   Crypted

But who defines each
situation? Our finance
committee vs. their
finance committee.

     Point. Click. Shoot.

          Wendy2: anyone see Derrick?
          aaron: NLG needs J-----'s birthday

❏ Reply
❏ Retweet
❏ Favorite

>So I am going downtown
>to attempt to get back
>my tent and Lindsey's
>paper cutter, not because
>I care that much
>about stuff, but I'm
>interested in the logistics.

As I am I because
the big state knows me.

As we press
up against the facts
such as they will have been
and from have-been to will
is the breach in function-
al time, where being
in public space with nothing
to do is something
to work with—instead
of killing time you're
free to live it, in it

        Can you bounce
        up and down?

    So I can find
    those yous
    that ache for-
            wards

these thrashing
thresholders

these, this,
this us

      Whose fuckups?
      Our fuckups.

      We watched
      as the construct-
      ion worker
      took a shovel
      to the shins
      of the celebrity
      architect.

❏ Reply
❏ Retweet
❏ Favorite

      Jack: j——r's 38. march 28

If representation
is nothing
more than
the ex-
tension
of context
into forms
testing content
& leaking matter

My hope then is that
by the time this is scanned
its affective logics
and self-ad-
ministered prosthetics
will have been

rendered obsolete
by the events to come.

Where   are   those   bicycle   scouts?

Text blast
system auto text:
Welcome back
to the system!

Point. Click. Shoot.

And so it's go time
in the illuminated
copter-lights, our bodies
flung up and slam
dancing in the after-gas
rhythm'd 'gainst
the chopper blades and
holding down the inter-
sections, not yet kettled
by the so-called
realism of the cynics
tweeting from the rapid-
ly shrinking sidelines
you can smell the auto-
nomy in the plaza
one part vinegar
to one part Maalox
to two parts tactical
action cannabis
you can't believe
your stinging eyes

but there we are,
our own audience—
lashing, lit and lit up
by the fires we set
to cast some shadows
to creep back into

Landscrapes of dis-
sensus composted
with the shit we've
swallowed for too long
topsoil for the perma-
nent autonomous zones
that each of us sign-
sings, because we are
all sound—everybod's body
a bullhorn, a long-range
poetic device, so
be heard and not scene-
ry, for in the stages
to come, this we
can only ever be
the we we will have
found in 2am'd affinity—
thriller mobs lurching,
bouncing up and down,
pushing pressing on,
up & 'gainst & through & toward
unimaginable tomorrows—

DISTANCE NOW CLOSED BETWEEN

Fyi, argus fueling up. Chp holding our spot. Upon our return, chp heading home, fog moving in and may be an issue. We will stay up as long as possible. Protestors throwing things Bwy ifo Rite Aid. Crowd size apx 600-700. Unlawful assembly announcement given. 16/Tel CHP vehicle had its rear window broken out and there is a weapon inside. 1200 blk of Bway protestors using dumpsters to make their own barricade. Unit took bottle at 14/Bway. Units have made 3.

Situation Update #40—- Operation FOP 25 OCT 2011 @ hours

Argus coming back up. Checked weather, should not be a factor. Unit took another bottle 14/Bwy, protestors moving barricades. 1300 blk of Franklin apx 300 protestors. Protestors advising if we give them the park back we can go home. Protestors threw a bottle and hit their own people. Then threw several more. Making announcements now. Deploying gas

iLOGISTICS

"what's been revealed

as living information"

         640 acres for sale
             primed / real

"At Cupertino
the ring-
        like building echoes

a history of centrally
planned churches:

an open court-
yard planted   with fruit
    trees replaces the church

        11.1 gal @ \$2.959 = \$32.85
        plus a qt of 10W-40

    's assembly   area and
personal computers set   in
    cubicles replace the chapels.

        corporate
        country
        on the gas
        station
        speakers:

Uniformly positioned
columns support
both the inner and the outer

      circumference of
      the structure, giving the façade
   a well-proportioned

   "attenuated masochism"
   high desert   strip mall

   IHOP   Chevron   Shell

      "that's what mental
        illness is"

rhythm.

      The building
   is the epitome of sym-
      metry, and from every angle
  it offers an   infinite
perspectival   loop.

      , a prison
    construction site—

      empty
      cement
      big box

      storage for

Jobs
was mourned

after his death as if

     Rialto quarry
     Ralph's Rite Aid
        Starbucks

      "and you're the mark"

    he were a pope,
  adding an even
greater sense
of import-

trailing a tanker
    trailer

  The air
 tastes of it, the ports
& the mall,   in the pipes, to the

     ance to
     Apple's
     building.

   When completed,
   it will be eminent-

     Helicopter crop
       duster

     packing peanuts
     float & swarm

ly visible—and re-
cognizable—

     across the highway

from satellites.

"a counterfeit map—
it does not depict
California"

It is both an icon
and a manifesto."

— And.   <double-click>

Parking lots.

The pentagon with softened corners
Ikea'd into a concretized think-piece

on a fully funded future
Nothing ventured, nothing

Sluiced.

almond farm
along the
aqueduct

If you own it
then you better put a ring around it

Operating Systems
in concrete and glass

photovoltaic panels

corridoricity   and

private
landing
strips.

      having burrowed through
      the abattoir—

      palm trees surround
      the exit ramp motels

      "retaining walls"

                    [insert map of Silicon Valley
                    Superfund sites]

         "California,   only moreso."

6:15   100845 14.6 gallons @   sunset
        through the West-
                  ley tire fire / "that's
             synthetic. Books—
        a second-hand experience."

Oh the glossy features. Oh the trending novels.

Drone delivery zip code schematics.

Bubble-wrap and packing tape.

"the envisioned map

of California, which is
spurious, fades out"

Such that the janitors strike at dawn

                              Saw a movie once where

                    Migrant server farmers.

               Taylorist self-
          actuarialism on the google
                         bus   work   station
                    piecemeal wage minus $5
                         latté status
          update: efficient / mood: add to cart

                    logistics (ours): gears & wrenches.

7:12 pm, unknown exit.
Stanislaw County

rain hits the baked
pavement, smells like

          toxic summer.

               PKD & Spicer skyping
               through the California ether
                              net—where?

          coming through
          the radio:

"the empire is the
codification of
derangement—"

DISTANCE NOW CLOSED BETWEEN

Situation Update #41—- Operation FOP 25 OCT @ 2223hours

Crowd regathering at 15/Franklin. Crowd of 300-400 at 15/Franklin moving to 15/Bway (main crowd of apx 300). Small group 15/Franklin. Crowd moving northbound. 15/Bway deployed gas, were taking bottles here. Crowd moving westbound 17/bwy. Crowd has taken over intersections at 17/Bwy. apx 300 protestors. Snow park has apx 20-30 protestors here. Crowd moving southbound Bwy per Argus, still blking all lanes of traffic. 14/Bwy masking up again, crowd is reacting. Protestors are verbally challenging units on the line.

Situation Update #43—Operation FOP 25 OCT @ 2342hours

Unites were taking bottles, deployed gas again. Trash can on fire at 1624 Franklin. 15/Bwy apx 50-60 protestors spread out here. 14/Bwy 75-100, small group at 14/Franklin also apx 40-50. Units advd no fire at 17/Franklin. MW 6'0 ponytail, heavy padding w/backpack approaching the line, units advd to mask up.

FIRE ON FIRE

"Fire is material-
ized time"—and

fire in the pure
present of the riot

form deforms cop
time (-and-a-half

for riot 'control')—
shit that burns

takes what time
to have been assembled

by whose hands, whose
fingers that now flick

lighters to light & make
light, flames against

the factory, the wage-hour—
all that is ether, even

labor-time itself, congealed
into flammable 'goods,'

tinder for "selfhood
in which light is

identical with heat"—
as embers—or sparks?

"'until a situation is created'"
in which the fire cannot be

contained. As "As in Zola
this set will foreground

social setting." Against what
field, what context &or con-

Maybe fill 'em up with petrol
to pour in th' empty bottles

we drained last night in reading
group, post-arguments and smokes

who brought the case of Applejack?
as in "percent that rolls their own"

He pissed into the flowerbed
We were all like, *dude,* bad form

#foregroundflora 's also
one kind of shout-out here

As in, shout out 3rd floor windows
or chuck some potted plants

at the pigs in line below
"percent respondents said"

As in Spivak, as in Biko,
as in Nineteen seven seven

as in sick-of, as in health food
stores, as soon-to-be

liberated champagne
livestreamed to the future

as with rough ranks, windsweep'd,
in crockpot photo bombs

Background mining rights,
foreground cobblestones

dude, you hurt my foot
droppin' so many names

78%—"as such"—
is an empty signifier

and yet today I'm feeling
alright about those 3/4

of friends with black bloc Bics
set to set against it,

to alight an "empty volume
of its own social facts."

78% of Bay Area evictions
78% of dot com capital

78% of Facebook posts
78% of Oakland cops

78% of downtown windows
78% battery power left

dude, that fire's 78% oxygen
so let's all fan the flames

but "fan the flames"
's an empty sign

if only signing f-i-r-e
outside its social setting.

I'm 78% convinced
that couplets are no curative

Background finance,
foreground formalisms

to burn that down with pleasure
with tinder lit, til anti-form'd,

to joyfully render the present
even more intolerable

by any memes necessary
to the conditions, Roger that,

at, as in CAConrad's words:
"no other speed than suddenly"—

or as in Wanda Coleman's:
"Fire! Fire! Fire! Fire! Fire!..."

(re the LA Riots, chanting,
as she left the building...)

Background "the conditions
themselves," foreground crying out

in deranged alphabets,
played on a burning piano

being pushed down the street
& into the conflagration

strings popping and snapping
like vocal cords lashing against

the ratio of oxygen to windpipe
as fire consumes the scream

sung out like shattered glass,
"a specific convulsion"—a

"counter-rhythmic interruption,"
rupturing time-sound, ground-waves

lower notes thunderclaps
upper notes songbirds in distress

"...crazy flowers / cry up across
the sky, spreading and hissing..."

Fire as "absolute unrest," unloosed
from regimented time, as in

Diamanda's broken heartsong,
glass that burns and melts

casts spells against the law
every night's the first of May

Toss broken flow'rs atop the pyre
til caustic flames sing out:

"Here is the rose.
Now we must dance!"

NOTES

This book was written in Oakland, beginning at the Occupy Oakland camp at Oscar Grant Plaza in October 2011 and through the irruptions throughout the Bay Area in the wake of the Trayvon Martin, Michael Brown, and Eric Garner (and, and, and, and...) (pseudo-)'verdicts' in 2013-2014.

My sincere thanks and appreciation to my friends and comrades within the recent overlapping radical and insurrectionary movements and moments, including the Oakland Poets Brigade, Juliana, Bill, Charles, Durback, Kenower, JClo, Jasper, Ali, Jami, Wendy T, Sophia W, Nico, Handsome Jack, Chris Chen, Timmy, Omar, Sri, Ayr, Aaron Begg, Oki, Eirik, Dereck, Jill Richards, Tim K, Brigitte, Bonal, Olive, Sara, ChrisM, Melvin, Tess, Jesse, Ben, Lalei & AntiRep, Boots, the FTP Assembly, the Feminist Vigilante Gang, the #ACAC19, the #J28 Committee, the #OO Medics, the Facilitation Committee, Nicole, Margaret, Jayo, Erin, SaraM, PunkBoyinSF, and so many others.

Thanks also to CAConrad, Marianne Morris, Sean Bonney, Abby Crain, Syd Staiti, emji spero, Tom Comitta, Homay King, Dodie Bellamy, Thom Donovan, Christian Hawkey, Stephen Collis, Anne Boyer, Donato Mancini, Cecily Nicholson, Aaron Vidaver, Bhanu Kapil, Rob Halpern, Dawn Lundy Martin, Matt Timmons, Jessica Tully, Roger Farr, Jules Boykoff, Frank Sherlock, Joe Luna, Lyn Hejinian, Michelle Naka Pierce, Anna Moschovakis, Brian Ang, Jena Osman, Will Rowe, and the many others I'm forgetting here.

Earlier versions of sections of this book (or sections of the project not included here) have been published in *The Brooklyn Rail, Floor, The Capilano Review, Boog City, Hi Zero, Poetry and Revolution, Esque, 580 Split, Shampoo, Armed Cell, Lana Turner, Volta, It's Night in San Francisco but it's Sunny* in Oakland, *Work*, *Capitalism Nature Socialism*, *The Journal of Aesthetics and Protest*, *Touch the Donkey,* and *Joyland Poetry*. Iterations of the performance pieces and talks folded into the book were tested at The Bowery Poetry Club, Small Press Traffic, the Poetry and Revolution conference (Birkbeck, University of London), Naropa College's Violence and Community symposium, Kadist San Francisco, and in and around Oscar Grant Plaza. My thanks to the editors, curators, and publications.

CLEARING A SPACE IN THE FREQUENCY JUNGLE (2013-14)
Includes language from Anne Boyer, Ronald Paulson's *Art of Riot*, and Nanni Balestrini's *The Unseen* (translated by Liz Heron), from which I culled the poem's title.

NOISE IN THE FACE OF (2014)
Includes language from Robbe-Grillet's *Project for a Revolution in New York* (translated by Richard Howard), Claudia Rankine's *Citizen*, Raoul Vaneigem (translator unknown), Courbet (translator unknown), and Habib Tengour (translated by Piere Joris). Title comes from (half) a line of Sean Bonney's.

HELLAGRAMS (2013-14)
Includes language from Jean-Luc Nancy (translator unknown).

WE DO THE POLIS (2011-13)
Includes language from Nat Raha, Ronald Paulson, and Hung Q. Tu.

WE FOUND LULZ IN A HOPELESS PLACE (2013-14)
For and after Jeff Derksen, Donato Mancini, Andrew Kenower, Matt Bonal, Anne Boyer, and the #OO/#FTP sound crew. Includes material/nudges from Caroline Bergvall, Miguel Gutierrez, Brecht (translator unknown), Robbe-Grillet,

Dionne Brand, Jereon Mettes (translated by Vincent van Ger-
ven Oei), Henri Lefebvre (translator unknown), Susan Parenti,
Eric Hobsbawm, Ingrid Burrington, Fredric Jameson, the
Carville Annex Instagram feed, overheard conversation, some
youtube video on surveillance and fashion, & who knows what
else.

EVERYTHING IS PIXELATED (2012-13)
Performance documentation. Conceptualized with collabora-
tion & choreography from Abby Crain. Syd Staiti edited the
video. In the performance at Small Press Traffic in SF, Abby
Crain was my co-performer. Part two is a version of a talk I
gave at Kadist in SF. Thanks to Abby Crain, Syd Staiti, Mi-
randa Mellis, & Joseph del Pesco.

A SWARMING, A WOLFING (2011-2012)
Includes material/nudges from Anna Tsing, Marianne Morris,
Anne Tardos, Leslie Scalapino, Lara Durback, DeWayne
Fraizer Dickerson, Jules Boykoff & Kaia Sand, The New
Pornographers, as well as material from a performance at
Naropa on Mayday, 2012 (as part of the "Violence and Com-
munity" symposium), in which I publicly live-wrote through a
classroom projector for three hours during the Mayday Gen-
eral Strike actions in Oakland, transcribing and restructuring
livestream reportage, tweets, and texts from Oakland. The title
comes from Deleuze & Guattari, discovered in an essay by
Olive Blackburn.

iLOGISTICS (2014)
Mash-up of material from *Art in America*, an audiobook of
Philip K Dick's *Valis*, and notes from a drive thru Central Cali-
fornia up the 5 back to Oakland. The quotations from Dick
were inserted into the text at the moment they were broadcast
from my truck stereo while driving home from Landers, CA
on October 31, 2008, the day after finishing *The Shunt* and
saying goodbye to poetry. For Juliana & Jasper.

FIRE ON FIRE (2016)
for/after Will Rowe, with additional language from Roger Farr,
Wanda Coleman, Sean Bonney, CAConrad, Yedda Morrison,
Aimé Césaire, Gwendolyn Brooks, Hegel, & Marx.

DISTANCE NOW CLOSED BETWEEN (2011)
Appropriated language from leaked internal City of Oak-
land/OPD emails from the night of the first raid of Oscar
Grant Plaza and the subsequent rebellion.

ROOF BOOKS
the best in language since 1976

Recent & Selected Titles

- FRANKLINSTEIN by Susan Landers. 144 p. $16.95
- PLATO'S CLOSET by Lawrence Giffin. 144 p. $16.95
- we plié by Patrick R. Phillips. 120 p. $16.95
- social patience by David Brazil. 136 p. $15.95
- PARSIVAL by Steve McCaffery. 88 p. $15.95
- THE PHOTOGRAPHER by Ariel Goldberg. 84 p. $15.95
- TOP 40 by Brandon Brown. 138 p. $15.95
- DEAD LETTER by Jocelyn Saidenberg. 98 p. $15.95
- THE MEDEAD by Fiona Templeton. 314 p. $19.95
- LYRIC SEXOLOGY VOL. 1 by Trish Salah. 138 p. $15.95
- INSTANT CLASSIC by erica kaufman 90 p. $14.95
- A MAMMAL OF STYLE by Kit Robinson
  & Ted Greenwald. 96 p. $14.95
- VILE LILT by Nada Gordon. 114 p. $14.95
- DEAR ALL by Michael Gottlieb. 94 p. $14.95
- FLOWERING MALL by Brandon Brown. 112 p. $14.95.
- MOTES by Craig Dworkin. 88 p. $14.95
- APOCALYPSO by Evelyn Reilly. 112 p. $14.95
- BOTH POEMS by Anne Tardos. 112 p. $14.95

Roof Books are published by
Segue Foundation
300 Bowery • New York, NY 10012
For a complete list, please visit **roofbooks.com**

Roof Books are distributed by
SMALL PRESS DISTRIBUTION
1341 Seventh Street • Berkeley, CA. 94710-1403.
spdbooks.org